SINGAPORE

THE CITY A[...]

ArtScience Mus[...]
Together with M[...]
behind it, also d[...]
blooming form (o[...]
unique structure symbolises new Singapore.
See p084

Marina Bay Financial Centre
The Kohn Pedersen Fox-designed mega-
complex — comprising office towers, shops
and apartment blocks — is the centrepiece
of a second, still-evolving business district.
Marina Boulevard

The Sail @ Marina Bay
Designed by Timothy Johnson and Peter Pran
of NBBJ, the city's tallest condominium tower
was inspired by a sail catching the wind.
Marina Boulevard

Clifford Pier
Once, immigrants landed here, but these days
the 1933 jetty houses The Fullerton Bay Hotel's
lobby and an upmarket Chinese restaurant.
80 Collyer Quay

The Fullerton Hotel
Opened in 1928, the former post and tax office
was restored to its full Palladian glory in 2000.
1 Fullerton Square, T 6733 8388

OCBC Centre
A reminder of the city's brief flirtation with
brutalism, IM Pei's 1976 concrete slab used to
be the tallest building in Southeast Asia but
has now been well and truly muscled out.
65 Chulia Street

Boat Quay
The epicentre of the old port, this row of mid
19th-century 'godowns' was converted in the
1990s into seafood eateries, pubs and clubs.

INTRODUCTION
THE CHANGING FACE OF THE URBAN SCENE

Time was when Singapore had a deserved reputation for being a soulless, air-conditioned metropolis. Its claims to fame were the shop-fest of Orchard Road and a list of banned activities, including littering and selling *Cosmopolitan*. The new Singapore still has the retail obsession and state control, but over the past decade it has transformed itself into a vibrant crucible of cuisine, art, sport and fashion. These are the best of times. The F1 Grand Prix is a fixture, the city regularly hosts the World Architecture Festival, and there's no better place to land, or depart, than super-handy Changi airport, regarded as the best on the planet, and a booming regional hub.

For a snapshot of Singapore's ambitions, look to the massive development on Marina Bay, where a glitzy casino resort appeared out of nowhere and a new CBD is in the making. The burgeoning restaurant scene, crowded with cash-rich locals and expats fleeing Europe's woes, is a stunning sweep of local flavours and pan-Asian techniques. The confidence that you feel on the streets is authentic, whether in the lively rooftop bars that seem to spring up every day, in the art hubs, the best of which is housed in an old army barracks, or in the bold new architecture by the likes of SCDA and WOHA.

Head out to Sentosa Island. Yes, the beach is manmade and the main attractions are Universal Studios and Resorts World Sentosa, but in the shrieks of excitement you can hear the future of this city-state: the sound of a buttoned-up people finally having fun.

ESSENTIAL INFO
FACTS, FIGURES AND USEFUL ADDRESSES

TOURIST OFFICE
Singapore Visitors Centre
216 Orchard Road
T 6736 2000
www.yoursingapore.com

TRANSPORT
Airport transfer to city centre
Shuttle buses to several hotels can be
booked at the airport. The fare is S$9
www.changiairport.com
Car hire
Avis
T 6737 1688
Metro
Trains run from around 5.30am to midnight
www.smrt.com.sg
Taxis
CityCab
T 6552 1111
Travel card
A three-day Tourist Pass costs S$20

EMERGENCY SERVICES
Ambulance/Fire
T 995
Police
T 999
Late-night pharmacy (until midnight)
Silver Cross Medical Centre
275a Holland Avenue
T 6462 2818

EMBASSIES AND CONSULATES
British High Commission
100 Tanglin Road
T 6424 4200
www.gov.uk/government/world/singapore
US Embassy
27 Napier Road
T 6476 9100
singapore.usembassy.gov

POSTAL SERVICES
Post office
2-2 Hitachi Tower
16 Collyer Quay
Shipping
FedEx
T 1800 743 2626
www.fedex.com/sg

BOOKS
A Guide to 21st Century Singapore
Architecture by Patrick Bingham-Hall
(Pesaro)
Can Asians Think? by Kishore
Mahbubani (Marshall Cavendish Intl Asia)
Singapore Shophouse by Julian Davison
and Luca Invernizzi Tettoni (Laurence King)

WEBSITES
Art
www.acm.org.sg
www.nationalgallery.sg
Newspaper
www.straitstimes.com

EVENTS
Singapore Biennale
www.singaporebiennale.org
Singapore Design Week
www.designsingapore.org

COST OF LIVING
Taxi from Changi Airport to city centre
S$35
Cappuccino
S$5.50
Packet of cigarettes
S$13
Daily newspaper
S$1.10
Bottle of champagne
S$120

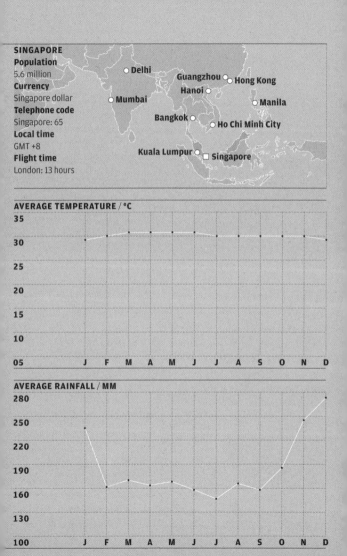

SINGAPORE

Population
5.6 million
Currency
Singapore dollar
Telephone code
Singapore: 65
Local time
GMT +8
Flight time
London: 13 hours

Delhi
Guangzhou
Hong Kong
Hanoi
Mumbai
Manila
Bangkok
Ho Chi Minh City
Kuala Lumpur
Singapore

AVERAGE TEMPERATURE / °C

35
30
25
20
15
10
05

J F M A M J J A S O N D

AVERAGE RAINFALL / MM

280
250
220
190
160
130
100

J F M A M J J A S O N D

NEIGHBOURHOODS

THE AREAS YOU NEED TO KNOW AND WHY

To help you navigate the city, we've chosen the most interesting districts (see below and the map inside the back cover) and colour-coded our featured venues, according to their location; those venues that are outside these areas are not coloured.

ORCHARD ROAD

Singapore's mini-answer to New York's Fifth Avenue, Orchard Road, which leads into Tanglin Road, is bookended by the venerable Regent (see p024) and WOHA's School of the Arts (see p081). The entire area is a shopaholic's dream of marbled emporiums and high-end boutiques like Off-White (see p090), as well as numerous five-star hotels. The vast ION Orchard (see p012), Paragon and Ngee Ann City malls are stomping grounds for the Prada set.

LITTLE INDIA

Atmospheric and cacophonous, Little India's labyrinth of roads and alleyways is infused with the smells and noise of Mother India, although it is considerably more sanitised. The streets teem with a bewildering array of silks, gold, spices, silverware and wood carvings, as well as boutique hotels such as Wanderlust (see p016) and unique stores, notably Onlewo (see p094). The South Indian restaurants here pack in the curry-hungry crowds.

TANJONG PAGAR

Few areas of Singapore can evoke as great a feeling of place and identity as Tanjong Pagar. Just south of the Singapore River, it boasts quaint reminders of the city's past. Elaborate Indian and Chinese temples and bustling markets jostle with bijoux stores and outré bars/nightspots such as Tantric (78 Neil Road, T 6423 9232) and Does Your Mother Know (41 Neil Road, T 6224 3965).

BALESTIER

North of Orchard Road, Balestier was once a bucolic retreat for the city's well-to-do. Today, it is a quarter full of historical and architectural landmarks. The main stretch, Balestier Road, wraps around the base of a low hill, taking in many of Singapore's finest colonial houses and the 1847 Goh Chor Tua Pek Kong temple (No 249), which has a freestanding Chinese opera stage.

RAFFLES PLACE

Taking its name from the country's colonial founder, Sir Stamford Raffles, the Central Business District, assembled around the mouth of the Singapore River, presents an extraordinary skyline. Some of the city's tallest skyscrapers, such as Kenzo Tange's UOB Plaza One (80 Raffles Place), rear up over Boat Quay's neat rows of old shophouses. Many of these have been converted into noisy (and rather touristy) discos, fun pubs, cafés and restaurants.

KATONG

This district remains one of Singapore's better-kept secrets. Whereas the rest of the island continues to obsess over shiny skyscrapers, Katong, nestled in the eastern suburbs, remains stubbornly anchored to a gentler past. The landscape comprises sedately ageing shophouses and bungalows, which host numerous excellent dining spots – try the Nyonya dumplings at Kim Choo Kueh Chang (60-62 Joo Chiat Place, T 6344 0830).

LANDMARKS

THE SHAPE OF THE CITY SKYLINE

Singapore is a small country: it takes barely an hour to zip from one end of the diamond-shaped island to the other. There's no real capital as such – the administrative headquarters, the parliament included, are scattered across the territory. However, most of the attractions and hotels are clustered in the south, notably around Orchard Road. A shopping and entertainment hub, it continues to grow – see the phallic tribute to consumerism that is ION Orchard (see p012). Further south is the CBD, bounded by historic Tanjong Pagar, and encompassing parts of Raffles Place and now Marina Bay. It's here that the skyline is changing the most, with expansion to the east anchored by KPF's Financial Centre (Marina Boulevard), and the domineering Marina Bay Sands (overleaf) – three 200m-tall skyscrapers topped by a giant surfboard, housing a hotel, a mall, a casino, a congress centre, a museum and myriad restaurants.

Yet just 10 minutes away is a necklace of rainforest and aerial walkways that begins at Mount Faber Park and winds through to Telok Blangah Hill Park (see p037). Out to the west are industrial estates and suburbs piled high with public housing; in the south are more green pockets like the Spice Garden at Fort Canning Park (River Valley Road). The north is sprinkled with reservoirs, and the east, dominated by Changi Airport, is an enclave of the Peranakans, descendants of Chinese immigrants and indigenous Malays.

For full addresses, see Resources.

Marina Bay Sands/Helix Bridge
Moshe Safdie's resort dominates Marina
Bay. The three towers are conjoined by a
cantilevered 12,400 sq m roof garden (see
p054) and resemble a huge three-legged
pi. The Helix Bridge, by Cox Architecture,
Arup and Architects 61, spans 280m and
offers pedestrian access, its steel bands
twisting in opposite directions like DNA.
10 Bayfront Avenue, T 6688 8868,
www.marinabaysands.com

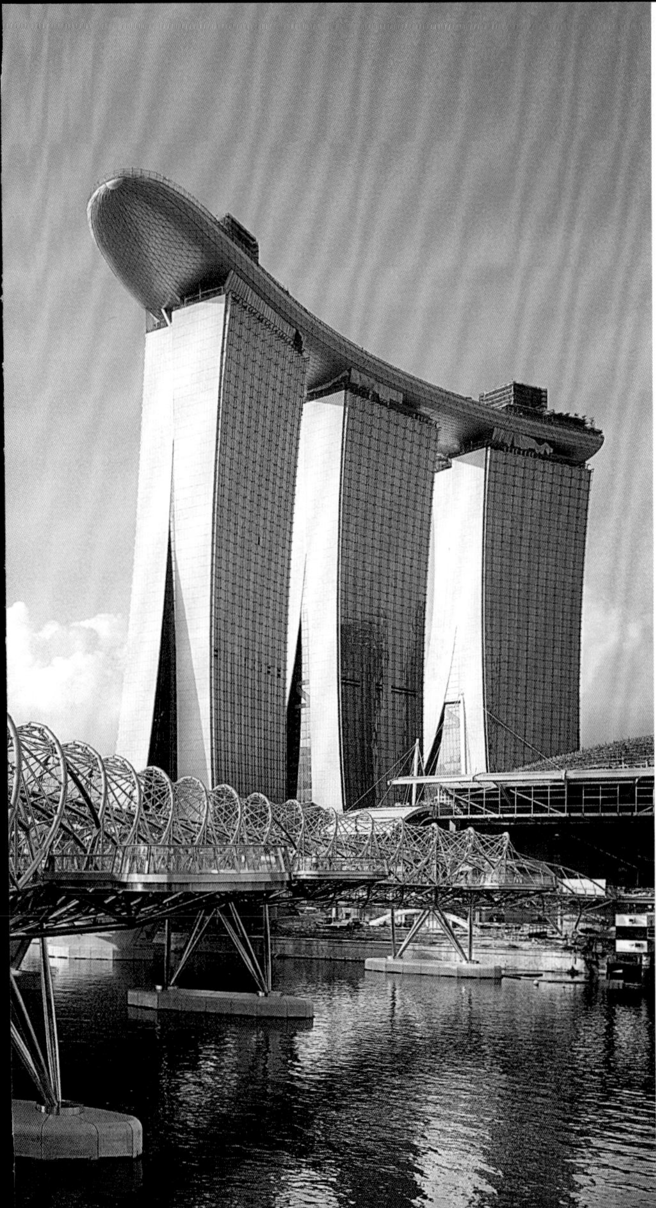

ION Orchard

Opened in 2009, ION immediately became an Orchard Road landmark. Its 218m steel-and-glass frame is supposed to resemble an upside-down tropical flower, although there have been less savoury comparisons. Designed by London-based firm Benoy, the structure's 'petals' – sheathed by a curtain of coloured lights – house 64,000 sq m of boutiques over eight levels, four of which are underground. The 'stem' (46 storeys of tony apartments) towers over the strip. There is also a substantial gallery that shows contemporary art. It connects to the Ngee Ann City mall (T 6506 0461) and Takashimaya department store (T 6738 1111) by tunnel, a common feature in this city, where the humidity and downpours mean that the great outdoors is a liability. *2 Orchard Turn, T 6238 8228, www.ionorchard.com*

People's Park Complex

In the 1960s, Singapore was in the throes of a modernisation drive as it struggled to relocate its population from overcrowded tenements while laying the foundation for an effective city plan on this tiny island. For architects, it was an exciting time as they experimented with concepts and solutions for mass housing and community hubs. DP Architects' People's Park, opened in 1973, was the first building in Southeast Asia to effectively combine residential, retail and office functions under one roof. Finished in raw concrete (now painted bright green and yellow), this brutalist statement was a laudable distillation of Corbusier's ideal of high-rise living, cleverly massing over a shopping mall podium to create 'streets' in the sky. It is still seen as one of the region's most important urban experiments.

1 Park Road, www.peoplesparkcomplex.sg

Pearl Bank

Towering above a flat neighbourhood of shophouses and low-rise office blocks, Pearl Bank has been a local icon since it was unveiled by architect Tan Cheng Siong in 1976. It was an innovative structure in a number of ways, not least for its unusual hollow circular shape. At 38 storeys high, it was also the tallest residential building in Asia at the time. To spread the load, Tan Cheng Siong arranged Pearl Bank's 272 apartments around 10 radial walls that rise through its entire height. Along with the support columns and the lift cores, this configuration facilitates the intricate stacking of the living spaces. A threatened sale (and therefore probable demolition) back in 2008 was narrowly averted after a concerted campaign by inhabitants and architectural conservationists.

1 Pearl Bank

HOTELS

WHERE TO STAY AND WHICH ROOMS TO BOOK

For years, Singaporean hotels have defaulted to a safe but bland marble-and-chintz look. However, the service is usually superior to their European equivalents, thus attracting Indonesian, Hong Kong and Taiwanese tycoons with their Gucci-clad wives. The large chains are mostly on or near Orchard Road, including the St Regis (29 Tanglin Road, T 6506 6888) and Regent (see p024), whereas the Shangri-La (22 Orange Grove Road, T 6737 3644) and a clutch of four-stars hold court on the arterial roads. Closer to the CBD is the legendary Raffles (1 Beach Road, T 6337 1886), as well as the Westin (12 Marina View, Asia Square Tower 2, T 6922 6888), with The Fullerton Bay Hotel (80 Collyer Quay, T 6333 8388) and Marina Bay Sands (10 Bayfront Avenue, T 6688 8868) right on the water.

More recently, hoteliers have been launching ventures in on-the-up Chinatown and Tanjong Pagar, where you will find the Anouska Hempel-designed Duxton Club (83 Duxton Road). In other districts, boutique properties include Hotel Fort Canning (11 Canning Walk, T 6559 6769), The Warehouse (320 Havelock Road, T 6828 0000) and Wangz (231 Outram Road, T 6595 1388), whose rooftop bar has fabulous views. The inimitable Loh Lik Peng brought some fun with Wanderlust (2 Dickson Road, T 6396 3322), while The Sultan (101 Jalan Sultan, T 6723 7101) and Hotel Vagabond (39 Syed Alwi Road, T 6291 6677) have dropped anchor in Kampong Glam.
For full addresses and room rates, see Resources.

Amoy Hotel

It used to be that Chinatown, despite its historical cachet and proximity to Raffles Place, was lacking in boutique hotels, so the Amoy was a welcome addition in 2013. Inspired by China's Zhengzhou people, who hailed from Amoy and settled in Singapore in the 19th century, the 37-room hotel is carved out of a row of shophouses and adjoins the 170-year-old Fuk Tak Chi, the city's oldest Chinese temple, which is now a museum. Rooms are furnished with an Asia-lite pastiche of silk brocade, daybeds, porcelain basins and calligraphy scrolls, and for an added quirk, are identified by Chinese surnames rather than numbers. The area's haul of superb restaurants and bars is a major draw, but do not overlook in-house Japanese diner JIN (T 6536 6258). *76 Telok Ayer Street, T 6580 2888, www.stayfareast.com*

Lloyd's Inn

In 2014, local outfit FARM transformed a
nondescript budget hotel into this 34-room
hideaway with a minimal, tropical modern
feel; tucked away behind a high wall, you'd
have little idea that bustling Orchard Road
is right on the doorstep. Indeed, the shady,
compact complex, which has a plunge pool
flanked by lush foliage, is reminiscent of a
set from *Saint Jack*, Peter Bogdanovich's
louche take on 1970s Singapore based on
Paul Theroux's novel. The spacious rooms
feature oak headboards and fixtures, and
concrete floors; we like the Big Skyroom
(above) for its tub en plein air. There is no
bar or restaurant, although the hotel's app
is a handy guide to the 'hood, and there's
plenty of communal space that includes a
sleek roof terrace, where you can BYO.
2 Lloyd Road, T 6737 7309,
www.lloydsinn.com

The Ritz-Carlton

Set in gardens on the edge of Marina Bay, The Ritz-Carlton is a byword for lap-it-up luxury. Designed by Pritzker Prize-winning architect Kevin Roche of KRJDA (the public spaces are by Howard Hirsch), the hotel is approached via a sinuous, green-canopied driveway. Guests step out into a 12m-high lobby of Italian marble, crowned by Frank Stella's spectacular *Cornucopia* (opposite). The common areas are like mini-museums, displaying more than 4,200 paintings and art installations, including pieces by David Hockney, Andy Warhol and Henry Moore. This has not come at the cost of comfort, however. Every room was made over by Burega Farnell in 2011, using a soft palette of pale timber, creamy faux-leather wall panelling and white marble floor tiles. We recommend Premier Suite 3126 (above), which has views over the Singapore Flyer.
7 Raffles Avenue, T 6337 8888,
www.ritzcarlton.com

Parkroyal on Pickering
Opened in 2013, Singapore's first green
hotel employs a host of eco initiatives
that fully exploit the city's abundance of
sunshine and rain: the property features
cascading vertical planting, waterfalls,
a wealth of shaded outdoor plazas and
solar-powered sky gardens, and harvests
rainwater. Local architects WOHA have
designed a light-filled 367-room oasis
(we suggest checking in to Room 1004
for its views of Hong Lim Park), furnished
in soothing green and woodsy hues. There
is also a wellness floor with a St Gregory
spa (T 6809 8870) and an infinity pool,
dotted with birdcage-like pavilions, that
looks out on the CBD. Allay jet lag with a
brisk walk around the verdant elevated
promenade that hems the exterior.
3 Upper Pickering Street, T 6809 8888,
www.parkroyalhotels.com

Regent

More than three decades old, the Regent continues to pull in a discerning business crowd who are drawn to its mix of sunny but understated service, locally rated restaurants and architect John Portman's soaring ziggurat atrium housing Michio Ihara's shimmering *Singapore Shower* sculpture (above). The rooms are dressed in neutral tones with an East meets West blend of chinoiserie furniture, Southeast Asian art, mustard-gold upholstery and L'Occitane products. Check in to Room 1133 for its satisfying views across the treetops along Orchard Boulevard. Dining options include the tempura at Tenshin (T 6725 3260), delicate dim sum at the renovated Summer Palace (T 6725 3288) and tasty Italian classics at Basilico (T 6725 3232).
1 Cuscaden Road, T 6733 8888,
www.regenthotels.com/singapore

Capella

In 2009, Foster + Partners, in collaboration with DP Architects, transformed an 1880s British military mess hall sited on Sentosa Island into a resort that is only missing a beach. This hasn't stopped the jeunesse dorée from flocking to its spa and open-air Bob's Bar (T 6591 5047), which overlooks three cascading pools (above). New wings with huge steel shades are hidden behind the original red-roofed mansion, and two officers' bungalows were converted into luxury three-bedroom Colonial Manors. Interior designer Jaya Ibrahim gave the 112 accommodations a low-key dose of Bali chic, using granite or marble in the bathrooms. All villas have plunge pools or jacuzzis, and Premier Seaview Room 410 has fantastic ocean vistas.
1 The Knolls, Sentosa Island, T 6377 8888, www.capellasingapore.com

The Club

Occupying a charming three-storey corner block, distinctive for its bold red shutters, The Club opened in 2010 and underwent a top-to-toe refurbishment by local design firm Distillery in 2015. There's a members-only vibe, from the public spaces hung with art and De Gournay wallpaper, to the 20 rooms with their muted wainscoting, woven vinyl floors and vintage furniture (Club Suite, opposite). Kick back in Mr & Mrs Maxwell's cosy lounge (T 6808 2181) or chow down in The Disgruntled Brasserie (T 6808 2184), where Daniel Sia dishes up mod-European fare like a foie gras beef burger and baked scallop tagliatelle. The secluded B28 basement bar (T 9298 8863) boasts around 200 single malts, although the prime seats are at rooftop Tiger's Milk (T 6808 2183), which serves fine piscos and views of the downtown skyscrapers.
28 Ann Siang Road, T 6808 2188,
www.theclub.com.sg

M Social
The 293-room M Social opened in 2016 at one end of buzzy Robertson Quay. The standard rooms are rather small — opt for a spacious loft or the Alcove Terrace (pictured), which has a courtyard — so Philippe Starck has employed a playful arsenal of peak ceilings, mirrors, glass, steel trims and low-slung furniture. The 31m-long infinity pool is a big help too.
90 Robertson Quay, T 6206 1888

Oasia Hotel Downtown

Local architects WOHA masterminded this green citadel that looms over Chinatown. Covered in vines and creepers, the red aluminium mesh facade has a variety of eco-friendly measures, including a series of sky gardens that cool the building and offset Singapore's often-oppressive heat. Apart from the lobby and dining venues, the hotel is set on floors 12 to 27, and these high-up oases are its best feature, replete with a yoga lawn and sun-dappled pools. Patricia Urquiola has accessorised the views in the 314 accommodations (Club Room, above) with low-hanging brass pendant lights and screens perforated with a stylised leaf motif. At street level, Cin Cin Bar (opposite; T 6385 2604) is a riot of turquoise and stocks 100 craft gins. *100 Peck Seah Street, T 6812 6900, www.stayfareast.com*

24 HOURS

SEE THE BEST OF THE CITY IN JUST ONE DAY

It used to be that 24 hours in Singapore was enough. Not now. You may have to crisscross the island a few times to get the most out of it but you'll rarely travel longer than 30 minutes. A trip out to the lush hinterlands (see p037), for instance, is illuminating, for some jaw-dropping housing projects (see p074) as much as the landscape, although the tropics have now been beamed into the heart of the city (see p036). Taxis are cheap and safe, if hard to find in the rush hour, while the MRT is super-efficient, and its network is growing.

The island's cultural mix is fascinating, and The Intan (opposite) and Chinatown Heritage Centre (48 Pagoda Street, T 6224 3928) offer a fine introduction. The government drive to turn Singapore into a regional creative hub continues, especially since the overdue arrival of a National Gallery (see p070), yet there's more of a buzz about the impressive complex of commercial galleries at Gillman Barracks (see p066). Afterwards, go for seafood in the conservatory at nearby The Naked Finn (39 Malan Road, T 6694 0807).

Then again, it's easy to eat well anywhere here. To sample local flavours, breakfast on soft-boiled eggs and toast with *kaya* (coconut and pandan jam) at Chin Mee Chin (204 East Coast Road, T 6345 0419), order dim sum at Swee Choon (183-191 Jalan Besar, T 6225 7788) or the swanky Summer Pavilion (see p035), and end the day with a Peranakan feast par excellence at Violet Oon (see p055). *For full addresses, see Resources.*

10.00 The Intan

To step into collector Alvin Yapp's home, set in a row of beautifully preserved early 20th-century terraced houses, is to travel deep into the heart of Peranakan culture. A private museum since 2010, The Intan holds an amazing collection of artefacts sourced from Penang, Malacca, England, China and India. These cover every single surface, although the space never strays into kitsch or clutter. Almost all aspects of Peranakan life are represented here, from carved ancestral altars to local teak furniture, ceremonial costumes, rare porcelain bowls, embroidered *kebayas* (traditional blouses) and beaded slippers. Yapp offers private one-hour tours that culminate in an assortment of Nonya snacks. Visits are by appointment only. *69 Joo Chiat Terrace, T 6440 1148, www.the-intan.com*

12.00 National Design Centre

Set up in 2013, the National Design Centre is a business and networking initiative for Singaporean creatives. For visitors, much of the interest lies in the architecture – a superlative conversion by native firm SCDA of a former convent school that occupied an elegant row of three heritage buildings and one Bauhaus-style block. The facade was restored, while the interiors have been reconfigured by adding a sculptural skylight to create a central atrium out of the old courtyard, and inserting a series of perforated aluminium and translucent glass boxes that interlock and cantilever to create shifting volumes and a sense of dynamism. The centre also hosts sundry independent ventures; seek out Kapok (T 6339 7987), a concept store and café. *111 Middle Road, T 6333 3737, www.designsingapore.org*

13.30 Summer Pavilion

A long-standing favourite with locals for its unimpeachable Cantonese menu, the Michelin-starred Summer Pavilion within the swanky Ritz-Carlton (see p020) was overhauled in 2015 by designer Tony Chi. The predominantly darkwood interior, featuring a rather fun carpet with Keith Haring-esque swirls, is well-lit by floor-to-ceiling windows that look out onto a bamboo garden. Executive chef Cheung Siu Kong's dim sum menu is a real treat, particularly the baked abalone puffs and deep-fried beancurd rolls, while mains are a fresh take on the classics, such as lobster poached with rice. The set lunches here are excellent value. Finish with one of the Tea Salon's artisanal blends, perhaps lychee oolong or black tea with white peaches.
The Ritz-Carlton, 7 Raffles Avenue, T 6434 5286, www.ritzcarlton.com

The Fall

15.30 Gardens by the Bay

The massive Gardens by the Bay complex, designed by UK-based Grant Associates and Wilkinson Eyre, is the latest salvo in Singapore's utopian rebranding as a tropical eco-city where blooming greenery enfolds 21st-century skyscrapers. Opened in 2012, the crown jewel of the three vast waterfront gardens is a 54-hectare twin-conservatory complex, dubbed Bay South Garden. Sheathed in steel and glass, the asymmetrical, ribbed biodomes are futuristic in their silhouette, their raison d'être revealed by glimpses of the plant life within, comprising more than 3,000 species from across the planet. The cool and misty Cloud Forest (above) houses high-altitude tropical flora clinging to the sides of a 35m-tall faux mountain. *18 Marina Gardens Drive, T 6420 6848, www.gardensbythebay.com.sg*

17.30 Henderson Waves

Singaporeans, never mind tourists, still think of their city as one giant glitzy mall and dining destination. Less known are the island's green spaces, especially the rainforest and mangrove swamps found in the centre, west and north. The National Parks Board has built a first-class network of walkways and bridges; a glorious jogging route. The Southern Ridges is a 10km trail through the parks of Kent Ridge, Mount Faber and Telok Blangah Hill. It crosses Henderson Waves, a 274m-long, 36m-high, snake-like pedestrian bridge. Designed by architects RSP using yellow bakau wood for the decking, the tops of the nine 'waves' form alcoves from which you can take in the view. The bridge itself is a fine sight at night, when it is illuminated by LEDs. *Mount Faber Park/Telok Blangah Hill Park, www.nparks.gov.sg*

20.30 Potato Head Folk

Occupying a pristine art deco building, this popular Chinatown haunt is an outpost of Bali's Potato Head Beach Club (see p097). At ground level, there is counter seating in the 'five-foot way' (a shaded corridor that is a common feature in buildings of this era) that's ideal for people-watching. On the first floor is Three Buns (above), one of the best burger joints in town; try the buttermilk-fried chicken burger. Further up the stairwell, which is decorated with whimsical murals (opposite) by Australian artist David Bromley, is the cocktail club Studio 1939, festooned with Chesterfields and rattan. On the roof, a surprisingly cool tiki-inspired bar serves a signature Saik Daiquiri mixed with Plantation 5 rum, mirin rice wine, yuzu, cane sugar and lime.
36 Keong Saik Road, T 6327 1939, www.ptthead.com

URBAN LIFE

CAFÉS, RESTAURANTS, BARS AND NIGHTCLUBS

Despite what Malaysians from across the Johor Straits might say, Singapore is without doubt a food mecca. The diaspora of youthful talent who returned from London, New York, Paris and Sydney in the late 20th century brought new culinary concepts; their menus now stretch from south Italian fare at Gattopardo (34-36 Tras Street, T 6338 5498) to modern takes on Peranakan classics at Candlenut (17a Dempsey Road, T 1800 304 2288), Japanese-influenced tapas at Bam! (38-40 Tras Street, T 6226 0500) and Southeast Asian small plates at Ding Dong (115 Amoy Street, T 6557 0189).

Street fare is unbeatable, and is available for a song in bustling coffee shops and open-air hawker centres in the suburbs. Entire quarters have their own specialities – sample traditional Nonya dishes in Katong, fish-head curries in Little India and pepper crab on the East Coast. Pick up the local Makansutra guide to hawker fare (www.makansutra.com) or visit the raucous Chomp Chomp Food Centre in Serangoon Gardens (20 Kensington Park Road).

Meanwhile, the city's nightlife scene belies its prissy reputation abroad. The storied nightclub Zouk (The Cannery, 3c River Valley Road, T 6738 2988) serves up a heady combo of electro and trance; Level 33 (Tower 1, 8 Marina Boulevard, T 6834 3133) boasts craft brews and giddy views; and the seductive speakeasy 28 Hongkong Street (28 Hongkong Street) is known for its original cocktails. *For full addresses, see Resources.*

Whitegrass

Opened in 2016 inside the 1841 Caldwell House in the grounds of Chijmes, a former convent overhauled into an entertainment hub, the Australian fine-diner Whitegrass is led by chef-proprietor Sam Aisbett. It is perhaps the most accomplished restaurant in the city, so indulge in one of the tasting menus. Delicately plated dishes might include scallops with purplish muntries, a berry from the outback, or Mangalica pork paired with abalone and lotus yam, followed by a dessert of young coconut mousse, jackfruit ice cream, longan and ginger cake. The interiors, by local outfit Takenouchi Webb, feature pastel-coloured midcentury-inspired furniture and brass accents, and overall meld a Scandi-driven aesthetic with a Bloomsbury set vibe.
1-26/27 Chijmes, 30 Victoria Street,
T 6837 0402, www.whitegrass.com.sg

Odette
At Julien Royer's Odette, a peach-hued, dream-like space, the culinary sleights of hand (mushroom tea poured over *cep sabayon* and slow-poached eggs scented with rosemary, for instance) are served underneath an installation of sublime floating forms by local artist Dawn Ng (see p062). Book a month in advance.
1-4 National Gallery, 1 St Andrew's Road, T 6385 0498, www.odetterestaurant.com

Jaan

Formerly helmed by chef Julien Royer (see p042), Jaan is now in the capable hands of Englishman Kirk Westaway, who delights with his modern French cooking. His menu puts emphasis on using first-rate produce sourced from speciality suppliers in dishes including Scottish scallops in a shellfish broth, and forest pigeon served on white polenta. He dresses up the classics too, such as a confit of rainbow trout drizzled with chicken jus. There's a 50-seat capacity beneath the dining room's rippling Murano glass chandelier, so do book ahead. The sleek New Asia bar (T 9177 7307), which is perched one floor up, has dizzying vistas. When you notice that the floor is tilting, don't blame it on your G&T; it slants at a 20-degree angle for a better panorama. *Swissôtel The Stamford, 2 Stamford Road, T 6837 3322, www.jaan.com.sg*

Stellar at 1-Altitude

Even in a city where venues jostle for 'best view' bragging rights, 1-Altitude's outlook over the skyline and the South China Sea is hard to beat. Take it in from the rooftop gallery, billed as the highest alfresco bar in the world; if you get a swaying sensation, even before a cocktail – perhaps the Tea Explosion, which blends gin, sweet sake, sour apple, rosemary, lemongrass and ginger tea – that's because the building's engineered to gently move with the wind. Designed by Ed Poole, the Stellar dining room, on the 62nd floor, is dramatised by sinuous metal sculptures that drop from the ceiling. In the kitchen, Christopher Millar prepares a progressive Australian menu with ingredients like Queensland Wagyu rib-eye and Japanese snow crab. *Level 62, One Raffles Place, T 6438 0410, www.1-altitude.com*

Hashida Sushi

Having charmed his way into the hearts of Singapore's sushi-philes, Japanese chef Kenjiro Hashida (or Hatch to his devotees) upgraded his eponymous restaurant to a 36-seat haute-cuisine establishment two floors up from his original digs inside the Mandarin Gallery, a glossy mall. The spare dining room is lined with blondwood and anchored by a silky smooth hiba counter that provides the stage for the exquisite *omakase* menus that revolve around the four seasons. Hatch first started learning his craft aged just 14 in his father's Tokyo restaurant, and it is mesmerising to watch him and his team carve slivers of marbled flesh from the belly of a huge bluefin tuna, or prepare delicacies like Ishigakigai clams, often flown in from the Tsukiji fish market. *4-16 Mandarin Gallery, 333a Orchard Road, T 6733 2114, www.hashida.com.sg*

Tanjong Beach Club

Opened in 2010, this secluded, sun-kissed throwback to 1950s beachside glamour was styled by nightlife impresarios The Lo & Behold Group. The place gives off a nostalgic vibe, and glass, wood and stone blur the lines between interior and exterior. The chic dining room dishes up tasty grilled meat and seafood, and the centrepiece outdoor bar is accented by hand-painted tiles. A 20m infinity pool, flanked by rows of daybeds, extends on to the beach where a mix of expats and local buff young things take in the sun while brazenly people-watching. Drop by on a weekend for a brunch of grilled fish, a signature Hollywood Punch (absinthe, rum, cold drip coffee, coconut water and pineapple juice) and a game of volleyball. *120 Tanjong Beach Walk, Sentosa Island, T 9750 5323, www.tanjongbeachclub.com*

StraitsKitchen

It cost a weighty S$7.5m to produce this slick, market-style restaurant, which was devised by Japanese firm Super Potato. Tucked away on the ground floor of the Grand Hyatt, the dramatic space features the interior design firm's trademark steel trim with timber and marble finishes. The menu runs the gamut of the island's varied cuisines, from Chinese (fried rice, noodles) to Indian (tandoori aloo, prawn masala) and Malay (beef rendang, satay). From behind a glass screen, the kitchen cooks up favourites, including traditional desserts such as *min jiang kueh* (pancake with grated coconut, red bean paste or peanuts). Some locals grouse at S$9 fruit juices and steep prices for the simpler dishes, but the crowds keep on coming.
Grand Hyatt, 10 Scotts Road, T 7632 1234, www.singapore.grand.hyattrestaurants.com

Chopsuey Café

For around two decades now, the PS Café
group has turned out one reliably stylish
establishment after another. At this 2013
outpost, located in an early 20th-century
army barracks, marble-topped tables and
rattan chairs complement the oversized
arrangements of tropical blooms and a
soundtrack of old Chinese jazz. As for the
menu, the restaurant's modus operandi
is telegraphed by its name, which nods to
the owners' penchant for Chinese fare
with an American spin. Expect short ribs
glossed with a sticky-sweet orange sauce;
eggs fried until bubbly and crisp, and
drizzled with soy; and a medley of plump
duck buns, prawn toast and satay sticks.
The cocktail list here is equally compelling,
not least the Mai Tai made with coconut,
chilli-infused white rum and lemongrass.
10 Dempsey Road 1-23, T 9224 6611,
www.pscafe.com

Horse's Mouth Bar

Finding the Horse's Mouth can be tricky. Either enter through a hidden door that adjoins a basement kaiseki restaurant, or at the bottom of the staircase of a ramen joint. However, the effort will be rewarded by a dark 43-seater izakaya and drinking den that designers Asylum have fitted with back-lit alcoves filled with 3,000 origami sakura flowers and shelves of mixed woods that resemble books. Early-bird diners swear by the tonkotsu ramen and sashimi, but it is the superbly crafted drinks that draw the post-prandial crowd. Purists will prefer the straight shots of sake and rare Japanese whiskies, but the cocktail menu constantly evolves. Try a Hadouken Sour, mixed with spiced rum, *umeshu*, lemon juice, brown sugar, bitters and egg white.
B1-39 Forum, 583 Orchard Road,
T 8188 0900, www.horsesmouthbar.com

Sky on 57

Native Singaporean Justin Quek made his mark with a decade of finely wrought French-Asian dishes at Les Amis (T 6733 2225), which opened in 1994 and is still going strong. In 2010, he launched this 57th-storey perch in Marina Bay Sands (see p010). The prized seats are on the terrace, with its vertiginous panorama, although diners with less of a head for heights will prefer to retreat into the enclosed dining room, an elegant and airy affair. Quek's classical French training is still at play, but it's the light Asian touches that make the place such a hit. Crowd-pleasers include *xiao long bao* (dumplings filled with broth and foie gras), ceviche dressed in truffle vinaigrette and a whole wok-fried Maine lobster in pepper sauce.
Marina Bay Sands, 10 Bayfront Avenue, T 6688 8857, www.marinabaysands.com

Violet Oon

Singapore's pioneering culinary star Violet Oon has written about the local cuisine for more than 50 years, both as a journalist and cookbook author. She opened National Kitchen (T 9834 9985) in 2015 inside the National Gallery (see p070), but we're still fond of her original establishment in Bukit Timah, although there is little to separate the two. Both dining rooms are lined with gilded dark wood, colourful wall tiles and black-and-white photographs. The menu is dense with classics from Oon's Peranakan heritage, from *ngoh hiang* (beancurd-skin rolls stuffed with pork scented with five-spice) to *buah keluak* (a bitter black nut from Indonesia) noodles. On a balmy night, try for a seat on the verandah, which is framed by potted plants and flame trees.
881 Bukit Timah Road, T 9781 3144, www.violetoon.com

Restaurant André
Fans of chef André Chiang flocked to this
beautiful Chinatown shophouse when he
opened here in 2010. There is artistry
throughout; from the paper-thin plates,
some of which are designed by Chiang
himself, to the signature eight-course
tasting menu melding French nouvelle
cuisine with Mediterranean accents.
41 Bukit Pasoh Road, T 6534 8880,
www.restaurantandre.com

Oxwell & Co

Ann Siang Road is experiencing something of a renaissance, its rows of restored fin de siècle shophouses now bristling with upmarket boutiques and restaurants, like Oxwell & Co. This high-ceilinged space is decorated with charm and flair by way of recycled furniture and vintage lights, but it's the cocktails and artisanal beers, siphoned through wooden kegs and a maze of exposed copper piping, that have made it such a success. Head bartender Luke Whearty makes standards with gusto and respect: the house gin and tonic is infused with fresh local nutmeg and homemade clove tonic water. Chef Nicholas Scorpion heads up the dining room (above), and sends out modern British dishes like ham hock terrine with mustard mayonnaise. *5 Ann Siang Road, T 6438 3984, www.oxwellandco.com*

OverEasy

The decor of this stylish bar/restaurant, conceived by designers Takenouchi Webb, pays homage to an American diner. There is red booth seating, a concrete and black-granite-topped bar that's backed by tinted mirrors, and veneered walnut on the walls and curved ceiling. Outside, the riverside terrace has stunning views of Marina Bay. From Wednesday to Saturday, the venue mutates into a fully fledged DJ lounge and cocktail bar – try the signature Breakfast of Champions (whisky, Dutch liqueur, maple syrup, lemon and a waffle biscuit). A supper menu of classic US comfort food, featuring cheesesteak sliders, haystack fries, milkshakes and mixed berry waffles, is served right up until 2am at weekends, so you've got no excuse to call it a night.
1-6 One Fullerton, 1 Fullerton Road, T 6684 1453, www.overeasy.com.sg

Open Farm Community

Singapore may be import-dependent, but Cynthia Chua has long been championing urban farming by supporting initiatives like Edible Garden City that are helping reconnect city-dwellers with the terroir. Her next move was to launch Open Farm Community, a restaurant set in a faux farmhouse on a bijou working property in the bucolic Dempsey quarter. Head chef Ryan Clift oversees imaginative dishes that are rustic and wholesome, and made with produce sourced from the grounds where possible, of course – try the coal-baked omelette with smoked haddock, or rigatoni tossed with mushrooms, smoked pancetta and stilton. A pre-prandial stroll through the papaya trees and a round of tabletennis or lawn bowls is de rigueur.
130e Minden Road, T 6471 0306, www.openfarmcommunity.com

Open Door Policy

In a city whose ethnic quarters can seem like Disney theme parks, there's a genuine vibe to the Tiong Bahru district. Among a fascinating mix of hawker stalls, Buddhist temples and early 1950s art deco-style flats, you will find the Spa Esprit Group's Open Door Policy, known as ODP by locals. Creative director Jerry De Souza has made the most of the deep, narrow space in this prewar shophouse, bouncing light off the embossed tin-lined ceiling and installing a glass-encased kitchen along one of the walls. The eclectic menu of international and Asian dishes is entirely gluten- and dairy-free, and there's also an unusually sophisticated coffee selection courtesy of 40 Hands (T 6225 8545), which is based across the road. Closed Tuesdays.
19 Yong Siak Street, T 6221 9307,
www.odpsingapore.com

INSIDER'S GUIDE

DAWN NG, ARTIST

Born in Katong, 'where you'll find the best coconut laksa noodles', Dawn Ng lives off Orchard Road. 'Yes, there are crowds yet it's so close to the lovely Botanic Gardens (1 Cluny Road),' she says. 'I love the idiosyncrasies of this island. And the food – who doesn't?'

On the way to her studio, she often stops at coffee roaster Chye Seng Huat Hardware (150 Tyrwhitt Road, T 6396 0609), where the *pandan gula melaka* pancake is a treat. On days off, she might head to Looksee Looksee (267 Beach Road, T 6338 8035), a tea salon and reading room curated by creatives, and next-door concept stores Supermama (see p089) and Scene Shang (263 Beach Road, T 6291 9629). She says not to miss the National Gallery (see p070), and its restaurant Odette (see p042), for which Ng dreamed up a canopy of hand-cut mobiles: 'It's a surreal experience for me to dine there.' She also likes Meta (9 Keong Saik Road, T 6513 0898), which serves French cuisine with an Asian twist, and the seafood palace Luke's (22 Gemmill Lane, T 6221 4468). On evenings out, she flits between Potato Head (see p038), 28 Hongkong Street (see p040), fun roof garden Loof (Odeon Towers, 331 North Bridge Road, T 6337 9416) and the hip Kilo Lounge (21 Tanjong Pagar Road, T 9824 9747).

Ng encourages visitors to take advantage of the cheap transport to explore. 'The evolving landscape and contrasting architecture tell the story of a country in the making, continuously reinventing itself.' *For full addresses, see Resources.*

ART AND DESIGN
GALLERIES, STUDIOS AND PUBLIC SPACES

No longer can it be said that the only reason to visit this city is to shop and eat. Over the past decade, the government has invested in soft power, from creative clusters like the Gillman Barracks (see p066) to the grassroots Design Centre (see p034) and a necessary institution, the National Gallery (see p070). Here you can see works that chart the emergence of the modern movement in the 1970s, leading on to Tang Da Wu's Artists Village, founded in 1988, the provocative acts by enfant terrible Vincent Leow in the 1990s, and an insight into those making waves today, including multimedia star Ho Tzu Nyen and ceramicist Jason Lim. Add to this a thriving independent scene, encapsulated by Gajah Gallery (see p069), and you'll find intriguing shows across the island at any given time.

There's art on the streets too, often by big-hitters like Botero and Dali sponsored by global firms, but also a few homegrown gems, in particular the legendary Ng Eng Teng's 1980 *Mother and Child* (Orchard Road/Cuscaden Road). And a busy calendar of sold-out events and fairs, which often champion regional talent, gives an idea of the deepening appreciation of the arts, as well as design, which is maturing due to pioneers like Nathan Yong (see p068). A recent trend has been to mine Singapore's rich Chinese, Malay and Indian heritage to give artisan and craft techniques a contemporary update, as seen at Supermama (see p089) and Onlewo (see p094). *For full addresses, see Resources.*

STPI Creative Workshop & Gallery

US master printer and publisher Kenneth Tyler opened this atelier in 2002 in a late 19th-century warehouse by the Singapore River. Since then, the STPI has become a world-class institution with its own paper mill, artists' studios and a large gallery. Guided by director Emi Eu, it explores the limits of paper and print – and tools like inks and oils – often using state-of-the-art techniques such as cyanotyping. Prominent figures from other disciplines are invited here on residencies to create pieces for its regular exhibitions. For instance, Japanese collage artist Shinro Ohtake showed 30 works, including expansive fluoro pulp paintings, for 'Paper – Sight' (above). 'It led to a big evolution for me,' said Ohtake. 'The possibility of realising new ideas.' *41 Robertson Quay, T 6336 3663, www.stpi.com.sg*

Gillman Barracks

It cost S$10m to transform a 1936 British army barracks in the Southern Ridges into the city's most exciting hub for Southeast Asian and global art. Opened in 2012, the complex now houses a dozen galleries, many of them major Asia-Pacific players like ShanghART, based in Shanghai and Beijing, Sullivan + Strumpf from Sydney, and Tokyo's Mitzuma Gallery, as well as the CCA (Centre for Contemporary Art), a space for collaboration. The FOST Gallery (above; T 6694 3080), set up by Stephanie Fong, champions local talent, from Tang Da Wu, seen as the father of Singaporean art, to emerging painter Eric Chan (*Slither*, above). Also in the grounds are restaurants and cafés, and design retailer Supermama (see p089). The bi-monthly Art After Dark events are wildly popular. Closed Monday. *9 Lock Road, www.gillmanbarracks.com*

Nathan Yong

Well before French furniture house Ligne Roset started producing Nathan Yong's 'Pebble' table in 2007, the designer was known for his unusual takes on familiar objects. In the years since, this sense has sharpened, seen in pieces like this chair (above) from his 2016 'Constellation' series. Upholstered in zesty velvets and trimmed in black marble, the clean lines call to mind art deco and Alexander Calder's mobiles, and lend the collection a weightless feel. It is on sale at Grafunkt (T 6336 6046), a stalwart of the design scene founded by Yong and Jefery Kurniadidjaja in 2009. Predominantly Asian brands are mixed and matched in a cheerfully chaotic loft-like space, while the house line GFNKT promotes imaginative work by up-and-coming locals, such as the 'Slot Bench'. *www.nathanyongdesign.com*

Gajah Gallery

Since it was launched by Jasdeep Sandhu back in 1996, Gajah Gallery has focused on Southeast Asia and, after expanding with a second outpost in Yogyakarta in 2015, has strengthened its representation of Indonesian artists. In Singapore, it is now set in an industrial warehouse on Keppel Road, and it's worth the schlep out to this cavernous venue. The 10 or so exhibitions a year invariably create a buzz, none more so than the 20th anniversary show, which featured 24 Gajah artists from both past and present. On display were iconic works by Semsar Siahaan (Indonesia) and Bagyi Aung Soe (Myanmar) beside new paintings by Ahmad Zakii Anwar (Malaysia), Li Jin (China) and Vasan Sitthiket (Thailand), in a comprehensive overview of the region.
3-4 Tanjong Pagar Distripark, 39 Keppel Road, T 6737 4202, www.gajahgallery.com

National Gallery

Singapore was seriously lacking an arts institution until the inauguration of the National Gallery in 2015. In conjunction with government arm CPG Consultants, Paris-based studioMilou preserved the neoclassical facades of the 1929 City Hall and the 1939 Supreme Court (pictured) and linked the two by draping a filigree metal-and-glass structure over the top. From some angles, this veil resembles finely woven rattan; from others, silky ikat. Inside, the old courtrooms, marble corridors and wood-panelled chambers have been integrated into a sequence of galleries housing the largest public hoard of contemporary art in Southeast Asia, including masterpieces by locals Lim Yew Kuan, Georgette Chen and Liu Kang.
1 St Andrew's Road, T 6271 7000,
www.nationalgallery.sg

ARCHITOUR

A GUIDE TO SINGAPORE'S ICONIC BUILDINGS

In order to fulfil government demands for a modern metropolis, planners spent the 1970s and 1980s razing whole swathes of art deco, colonial and Peranakan buildings to make way for Housing & Development Board towers, and now more than 80 per cent of the 5.6m population lives in these subsidised flats. Common sense has since prevailed, fortunately, resulting in a coordinated effort to preserve the built heritage, and seen in flawless renovations such as Baba House (157 Neil Road, T 6227 5731), and Architects 61's reimagining of Frank Dorrington Ward's 1933 People's Association HQ (9 King George's Avenue). It's a delicate balancing act between innovation and conservation, but for a city that has always been in a hurry to meet its future, Singapore is not losing sight of its past.

Thankfully, there has also been a shift away from the faceless functionalism of early public housing towards one-offs on a humane scale, exemplified by SkyTerrace (see p078). In the private sphere, considered projects like Paul Rudolph's 1994 The Concourse (300 Beach Road), an inverted pagoda, are no longer the exception. There has been a succession of superlative schemes since 2015, from The Interlace (see p074) to Moshe Safdie's Sky Habitat (7-9 Bishan Street 15), all stepped terraces and flying bridges, Jean Nouvel's Le Nouvel Ardmore (1a Ardmore Park), with its grids and recesses, and Zaha Hadid's rippling D'Leedon (Leedon Heights). *For full addresses, see Resources.*

AXA Life Building

There are now more than 700 buildings in the city that top 25 storeys. Sadly, many of them are unremarkable for anything except their height, so it's not surprising that very little attention has been paid to Singapore's early, more modest attempts at the high-rise. This 1974 headquarters for the city-state's largest building society, designed by local firm James Ferrie and Partners as the Wing On Life Building, is an understated gem, not least because it was one of Singapore's first energy-efficient structures. At a relatively lowly 64m, it is now dwarfed by the more contemporary developments on Cecil Street, and is easy to miss. Yet as a snapshot of the country's doomed flirtation with elegant tropical modernism – all concrete brise-soleil and slimline proportions – it is hard to beat.
150 Cecil Street

The Interlace
One of Ole Scheeren's last projects for
OMA, this inspired architectural jigsaw is
framed by the green Southern Ridges. A
series of 31 six-storey blocks, stacked up
to four high, is angled, cantilevered and
interlocked in a rough hexagonal plan,
enabling a surfeit of leisure space across
various levels, and encompassing 1,040
condo units with no sense of crowding.
184 Depot Road, www.theinterlace.com

Wowhaus at the Niven Road Studio

Architects Maria Warner Wong and Chiu Man Wong bought a midcentury shophouse on Niven Road in 1996 with the intention of redeveloping it into a live/work space. A 2003 heritage listing scuppered that, so instead they turned it into a collaborative hub for their peers – and named it after an amalgamation of their firm, Wow, and the Bauhaus movement. They exposed the original red-brick walls and the underbelly of the terracotta-tiled roof, and added a dramatic intervention at the rear with an extra entrance. Peeking cheekily over the roofline (above), the three-storey glass-and-concrete extension encompasses a basement and an attic, and is shaded by vertical fins (opposite). The building hosts ad hoc exhibitions, some of which are open to the public, others by appointment.
23 Niven Road, T 6333 3328, www.wow.sg

SkyTerrace@Dawson
Architects SCDA's SkyTerrace, together
with WOHA's nearby SkyVille@Dawson, is
a zenith in the city's ongoing experiment
with high-density public housing. The
five towers, finished in 2015, boast sky
gardens and yoga pavilions, while there
are double-height ceilings in many of the
758 units to allow compartmentalisation
for multi-generational communal living.
90 Dawson Road

Church of St Mary of the Angels

In 2003, at a time when many thought that there could be few surprises left on the local architectural scene, WOHA unveiled this beautiful church on the wooded slopes of Bukit Batok. One of their finest works, up there alongside the later MRT stations Bras Basah and Stadium, and the School of the Arts (1 Zubir Said Drive), the church is a graceful meditation on space on a vast scale, yet retains an unexpected intimacy.

The vaulted eyrie of the main prayer hall is lined with white-oak benches and lit by a forest of giant candelabra, and the light-drenched columbarium (above), a room where funeral urns are kept in recesses in the walls, is spectacular. There are also 12 reflection pools, a friary, offices and an apartment block for priests of the parish. *5 Bukit Batok East Avenue 2, T 6567 3896, www.stmary.sg*

Learning Hub, NTU

Heatherwick Studio's extraordinary design for the 2015 Learning Hub at the Nanyang Technological University (NTU) is a bold deconstruction of the traditional teaching set-up. Also known as The Hive, but soon nicknamed 'The Dim Sum' by students for its likeness to a pile of steamer baskets, a cluster of 12 eight-storey towers comprises 56 rough-hewn concrete pods – circular classrooms that help break down barriers between professor and pupil. These open into an atrium with clear sightlines up to the skylight and down to the plaza. There are almost no straight edges, whether in the undulating walls, cast with Aztec-like motifs, or the slanted load-bearing pillars that resemble tree trunks. Elsewhere on the NTU campus, the School of Art, Design and Media has a spiralling turfed roof that rises up from ground level to sweep over three glass blocks like a flying golf fairway.
52 Nanyang Avenue, www.ntu.edu.sg

ArtScience Museum

Even seen from a distance, Moshe Safdie's singular all-white structure on the edge of Marina Bay is an eye-catching beauty. Its 10 spheroid sections of varying height, all topped by a skylight, reach up to 60m, and are said to assume the form of either a lotus flower or a human hand. Inside, the curvilinear space wraps around a central oculus and a waterfall feeds an interior pool. Opened in 2011, the 21 galleries on three levels display exhibitions based on the concept of the interplay between art and science, for instance, a retrospective on MC Escher, and a series of seven films by Southeast Asian auteurs on the theme of water. Afterwards, treat yourself to a cocktail or two at Sky on 57 (see p054) in the nearby Marina Bay Sands (see p010). *10 Bayfront Avenue, T 6688 8868, www.marinabaysands.com*

Supreme Court

Behind its former Palladian digs (see p070) and opposite the squat Parliament House (1 Parliament Place), the new Supreme Court was Foster + Partners' second work in Singapore, completed five years after the 2000 Expo MRT station (21 Changi South Avenue 1). The interiors are suitably lofty, notably the atrium, and call to mind London's Canary Wharf station. The Court of Appeal, the country's highest judicial authority, sits in a Starship Enterprise-like dome (above), which, like the cupola of his Reichstag in Berlin, includes a wraparound viewing platform. Opinion is split between those who deride the sci-fi form, and local Foster-ites, who have since been further treated to Capella (see p025) and the eco-friendly South Beach (30 Beach Road).
1 Supreme Court Lane, T 6336 0644, www.supremecourt.gov.sg

Assyafaah Mosque
Forum Architects' mosque deliberately defies convention to attract all creeds: there is no dome, and the minaret is a sculpture of curved steel. The prayer hall (pictured) makes a grand statement, with its eight concrete arches and arabesque screens that blur the interior/exterior divide, and a four-storey slanted white marble wall inscribed with Koranic script.
1 Admiralty Lane, T 6756 3008

SHOPS

THE BEST RETAIL THERAPY AND WHAT TO BUY

There was a time when shopping here was confined to the glossy stores on the Orchard Road belt, and the selection was limited to clothing, accessories and electronics. All this still exists, of course. The air-con, labyrinthine malls are very much alive and well, led by ION Orchard (see p012), 313 Somerset (313 Orchard Road, T 6496 9313) and Knightsbridge (270 Orchard Road, T 6593 6999), but now the choice is more sophisticated, due to original concepts like K+ (3-11 Scotts Square, 6 Scotts Road, T 6694 8896), a 'Noah's ark' of local art, craft and design that hosts rotating pop-ups.

Meanwhile, many retailers have forsaken the high rents of this strip entirely, for Purvis Street, Haji Lane, Beach Road (opposite), Ann Siang Hill and Club Street, exemplified by MYthology (No 88, T 6223 5570), which carries independent fashion labels from across Asia. Chinatown and Little India are havens for antiques, but you will also find a modern reworking of history at Onlewo (see p094). There are more gems in the Holland Village enclave, notably Bynd Artisan (see p092) and Atelier Ong Shunmugam (43 Jalan Merah Saga 1-76, T 6252 2612), where traditional techniques and styles are mined to create immaculately tailored contemporary womenswear. Just down the road, Dover Street Market (18 Dempsey Road) was a headline launch in 2017. If you're out this way, stop for lunch at Chopsuey Café (see p050) or Open Farm Community (see p060). *For full addresses, see Resources.*

Supermama

When Supermama co-founder Edwin Low devised a slick range of ceramics that paid homage to everyday life, he couldn't have imagined how popular it would become, especially among homesick expats abroad. Designs by locals are fired on to saucers, plates and chopstick rests manufactured in striking blue and white by the Japanese firm Kihara. Best-sellers include 'HDB' by Chang Shian Wei (a stylised silhouette of public-housing balconies) and 'Otter' by Wan Xiang Lee (above), S$30, a collab with the Organisation of Illustrators Council. Supermama, which Low runs with his wife Mei Ling, also purveys fashion, homewares and accessories by Singaporean creatives, all made by artisans in Japan, in a minimal light-flooded store that's helping turn this pocket of Bugis into a top retail destination. *265 Beach Road, www.supermama.sg*

Off-White

Creative director Virgil Abloh established this Singapore outpost (there are stores in Hong Kong and Tokyo), in partnership with local retailer Surrender (T 6733 2130), for his brand Off-White in 2016. Subtitled 'Windows', for no apparent reason, the interior was designed by New York studio Family, who installed textured concrete walls, glossy floors, clerestory windows and Barrisol ceiling lights. It effortlessly melds luxury with grit, a concept Abloh embraces in his bold collections of made-in-Milan streetwear with a high-fashion edge, which often features his signature stripes. Menswear includes artfully beat-up bombers and plush sweatpants, while women are catered for with embroidered satin jackets and distressed denim pieces. Accessorise with leather hiking boots, slip-on sneakers and spray-painted backpacks. *268 Orchard Road 1-1, T 6702 1313, www.off---white.com*

Bynd Artisan

This charming little company, based in a quiet residential street in Holland Village, traces its origins back 75 years to a small book-bindery started by Koon Song Chan. These days, his granddaughter, Winnie Chan, has harnessed the know-how of the family atelier and its troupe of experienced craftsmen to create simple, natty lifestyle accessories for her company Bynd Artisan. Wares include travel wallets, book jackets, iPad cases, diaries, greeting cards, desk sets, luggage tags, and hand-stitched leather journals, which can be customised with a choice of paper, rivets and eyelets, and personalised with initials, as can most of the items. The devotion to artisanship extends to collaborations with local talent such as young calligrapher Joanne Lim. *44 Jalan Merah Saga 1-54, T 6475 1680, www.byndartisan.com*

In Good Company

Tailor Sven Tan and draper Kane Tan, along with two close friends, established In Good Company in 2012. It's a mostly cream-hued, airy space with concrete floors and black powder-coated racks in the basement of a mall. The on-the-up label is known for its contemporary cuts, flattering fits and a fresh, bright palette. Smart fabrics (fine cotton jersey, crepe) are combined with precise detailing like asymmetrical hems and exaggerated cuffs to create a line of understated staples. You'll also find craft jewellery, often produced in conjunction with local makers such as Argentum, that incorporates materials including glossed resin, ribbons, earthy-coloured leather and various metals. Refuel with pastries and coffee at the in-house Plain Vanilla bakery.
1-6 ION Orchard, 2 Orchard Turn,
T 6509 4786, www.ingoodcompany.asia

Onlewo

Owner Mike Tay's studio and showroom, Onlewo, is located on the ground floor of a shophouse in the historic Jalan Besar quarter. Its stock of retro-chic prints has made it a firm favourite with homeowners and interior designers alike. Tay's evocative sketches of the island's neighbourhoods, Peranakan culture and classic architecture grace a selection of soft furnishings and accessories from cushions to wallpapers, sofas and lampshades. The appeal lies in the blend of bold graphics and quirky local sensibilities, as traditional window grilles, Chinese opera singers and *kuehs* (bite-sized desserts) get a stylish pop art update. Upstairs is Flaneur, a contemporary art gallery that Tay co-founded with Vincent Chow to promote city-based artists.
129 Jalan Besar, T 9112 4685,
www.onlewo.com

Tarte

The austere interior is the first clue that Tarte is no ordinary patisserie. The second is that it's run by Cheryl Koh, who is the pastry chef at the much-laurelled Les Amis (see p054) restaurant around the corner. A certified star on the dessert scene, Koh and her team handmake her legendary tarts with French butter in small batches throughout the day. Showcased on a sleek marble counter, delicacies are decorated with seasonal fruits like Indian Alphonso mangoes, Japanese yuzu and plump figs. The sweets can either be packaged up in brightly coloured boxes or consumed in the Caveau Bar (T 6737 2622) next door, paired with coffee or wine. At weekends, Koh fills out the shelves with cream puffs and eclairs, as well as seasonal jams.
1-12 Shaw Centre, 1 Scotts Road, T 6235 3225, www.tarte.com.sg

ESCAPES

WHERE TO GO IF YOU WANT TO LEAVE TOWN

Singapore's location at the heart of Southeast Asia makes it easy to depart for a quick change of scenery. For instance, Phnom Penh is kicking off the emotional shackles of its troubled past with an exciting combination of smart restaurants, contemporary art and film festivals, against a landscape of beautifully restored colonial architecture and a riverfront flecked with seagulls. It also helps that price wars between the budget airlines have spilled over to the bigger boys' territory – these days it is not uncommon to find newspaper or online adverts for S$20 return flights to Phuket.

As so many destinations are only an hour or two away by plane, choices are innumerable. Short breaks are tempting all over the region – from Bali (opposite), whose many-splendoured charms include the eco-friendly Soori (Banjar Dukuh, Desa Kelating, T +62 361 894 6388), to Malaysian capital Kuala Lumpur (see p099), for its bustling nightlife and insanely good cuisine. Many well-heeled locals take weekends in Phuket (see p098); others, armed with a strong Singaporean dollar, nip up to Bangkok, or further afield to Tokyo and Seoul, for retail therapy and a culinary adventure. But before you start packing your other Wallpaper* City Guides into an overnight bag, don't forget there are some great places to explore in Singapore itself, such as the island of Pulau Ubin, for a taste of what this corner of the world looked like a century ago.

For full addresses, see Resources.

Katamama, Bali

Located on one of Seminyak's last prime stretches of sand, the 58-suite Katamama opened in 2016 as the first salvo in a mega-development by the Indonesian Potato Head group (see p038) that will comprise two more hotels, designed by Marcio Kogan and Rem Koolhaas. Here, architect Andra Matin has created a gorgeous symphony in red Balinese brick, along with handmade Javanese tiles and terrazzo, and Singapore firm Takenouchi Webb's interiors ooze West Coast midcentury cool, with lashings of teak. At the neighbouring Potato Head Beach Club (T +62 361 473 7979), languid days around the infinity pool segue into a sundown party vibe as global DJs crank up the tunes. To get here, it is a three-hour flight and then a short drive up the coast. *51b Jalan Petitenget, Seminyak, T +62 361 302 9999, www.katamama.com*

The Residences by Anantara, Phuket

Located within the Anantara Layan Phuket Resort, The Residences are split-level villas terraced into a low hill overlooking a cove in the Sirinath National Park. In one of his last projects, designer Jaya Ibrahim drew from an Asia-lite moodboard, and interiors feature carved ceilings, Thai travertine and terrazzo floors, embellished by handwoven rugs, bronze lamps and ceramics. Each pad has from two to seven bedrooms and a 21m infinity pool (above) with views over the Andaman Sea — a vantage point perhaps only trumped by the rooftop deck. A chef and butler are at your beck and call, while resort amenities include yacht charter, a wellness centre and two restaurants. It is a two-hour flight to Phuket in Thailand, where you will be picked up by limousine. *168 Moo 6, Layan Beach Soi 4, T +66 76 317 200, www.phuket-layan.anantara.com*

Kuala Lumpur, Malaysia

It's just an hour's hop to Singapore's arch rival KL. Its defining landmark, Cesar Pelli's 450m Petronas Twin Towers, briefly the world's tallest building, provides a striking reminder that the region's city of the future has already arrived. Yet the capital does have some less brash gems. Designed by the Public Works Department, the 1965 National Mosque (above) was a watershed in the modernist movement. The prayer hall is housed under a flat 16-point star that fans out like a concertina, and spaces are linked by wide galleries with perforated screens that provide ventilation. Do not miss the Islamic Arts Museum (overleaf), either. Its global collection of artefacts is laid out in a white marble mansion with high clerestories, fountains and turquoise-hued domes. Stay the night in the rather stylish Hotel Maya (T +60 3 2711 8866).

Macalister Mansion, Penang

This little island in north-west Malaysia, an 85-minute plane ride from Singapore, is undergoing a renaissance. Long famed for its incredible food, it's crowded with attractive British colonial architecture, Buddhist temples and, today, a clutch of hipster hotels. Book into the Macalister Mansion, which launched in 2012 and is named after the former governor – a grand fin de siècle pile given a facelift by Colin Seah of Ministry of Design. While sympathetically preserving the original detailing, Seah has treated each room to a unique look by installing features such as sculptural art, chrome canopies and iron spiral staircases. The Living Room (above) offers a casual dining space, but there is no scrimping on the flavours.
228 Macalister Road, George Town, T +60 4 228 3888, www.macalistermansion.com

Amansara, Siem Reap

Two hours' flight from Singapore in north-west Cambodia, Siem Reap is the gateway to the ancient capital of the Khmer empire. Once a party hangout for King Sihanouk, the 1962 villa was designed by Frenchman Laurent Mondet and is one of the finest examples of midcentury architecture in the country. After a sensitive conversion into the Amansara by Singapore-based Kerry Hill, its splendour remains undiminished, from the flat canopy roofs to the singular pool and circular dining room; Pool Suites best capture its understated elegance. An army of tuk-tuks zip guests to Angkor Wat in minutes. Best seen at dawn, the 900-year-old temple is part of an astounding trove of religious sites, civic structures and reservoirs spread over a vast 400 sq km. *Road to Angkor, T +855 63 760 333, www.aman.com/resorts/amansara*

NOTES
SKETCHES AND MEMOS

RESOURCES
CITY GUIDE DIRECTORY

HOTELS

ADDRESSES AND ROOM RATES

Amansara 103
Room rates:
double, from USD$1,250
Road to Angkor
Siem Reap
Cambodia
T +855 63 760 333
www.aman.com/resorts/amansara

Amoy Hotel 017
Room rates:
double, from S$370
76 Telok Ayer Street
T 6580 2888
www.stayfareast.com

Capella 025
Room rates:
double, from S$1,050;
Premier Seaview Room 410, S$1,250;
Colonial Manor, from S$19,000
1 The Knolls
Sentosa Island
T 6377 8888
www.capellasingapore.com

The Club 026
Room rates:
double, from S$230
28 Ann Siang Road
T 6808 2188
www.theclub.com.sg

The Duxton Club 016
Room rates:
prices on request
83 Duxton Club
www.starwoodhotels.com

Hotel Fort Canning 016
Room rates:
double, from S$550
11 Canning Walk
T 6559 6769
www.hfcsingapore.com

The Fullerton Bay Hotel 016
Room rates:
double, from S$550
80 Collyer Quay
T 6333 8388
www.fullertonbayhotel.com

Katamama 097
Room rates:
double, from USD$300
51b Jalan Petitenget
Seminyak
Bali
T +62 361 302 9999
www.katamama.com

Lloyd's Inn 018
Room rates:
double, from S$160;
Big Skyroom, from S$270
2 Lloyd Road
T 6737 7309
www.lloydsinn.com

M Social 028
Room rates:
double, from S$150;
Alcove Terrace, from S$200
90 Robertson Quay
T 6206 1888
www.msocial.com.sg

Macalister Mansion 102
Room rates:
double, from S$290
228 Macalister Road
George Town
Penang
Malaysia
T +60 4 228 3888
www.macalistermansion.com

Marina Bay Sands 016
Room rates:
double, from S$680
10 Bayfront Avenue
T 6688 8868
www.marinabaysands.com

Hotel Maya 099
Room rates:
double, from USD$100
138 Jalan Ampang
Kuala Lumpur
Malaysia
T + 60 3 2711 8866
www.hotelmaya.com.my

Oasia Hotel Downtown 030
Room rates:
double, from S$550;
Club room, from S$660
100 Peck Seah Street
T 6812 6900
www.stayfareast.com

Parkroyal on Pickering 022
Room rates:
double, from S$340;
Room 1004, from S$440
3 Upper Pickering Street
T 6809 8888
www.parkroyalhotels.com

Raffles 016
Room rates:
double, S$750
1 Beach Road
T 6337 1886
www.raffles.com

Regent 024
Room rates:
double, from S$225;
Room 1133, from S$380
1 Cuscaden Road
T 6733 8888
www.regenthotels.com/singapore

The Residences by Anantara 098
Room rates:
Two-bedroom villa, from USD$3,000
168 Moo 6
Layan Beach Soi 4
Phuket
Thailand
T +66 76 317 200
www.phuket-layan.anantara.com

The Ritz-Carlton 020
Room rates:
double, from S$1,000;
Premier Suite 3126, from S$1,350
7 Raffles Avenue
T 6337 8888
www.ritzcarlton.com

Shangri-La 016
Room rates:
One room villa, from S$675
22 Orange Grove Road
T 6737 3644
www.shangri-la.com/singapore/shangrila

Soori Bali 096
Room rates:
double, from S$800
Banjar Dukuh
Desa Kelating
Kerambitan
Tabanan
Bali
T +62 361 894 6388
www.sooribali.com

St Regis 016
Room rates:
double, from S$500
29 Tanglin Road
T 6506 6888
www.stregissingapore.com

The Sultan 016
Room rates:
double, from S$150
101 Jalan Sultan
T 6723 7101
www.thesultan.com.sg

Hotel Vagabond 016
Room rates:
double, from S$230
39 Syed Alwi Road
T 6291 6677
www.hotelvagabondsingapore.com

Wanderlust 016
Room rates:
double, from S$300
2 Dickson Road
T 6396 3322
www.wanderlusthotel.com

Wangz Hotel 016
Room rates:
double, from S$500
231 Outram Road
T 6595 1388
www.wangzhotel.com

The Warehouse Hotel 016
Room rates:
double, from S$225
320 Havelock Road
T 6828 0000
www.thewarehousehotel.com

Westin 016
Room rates:
double, from S$350
12 Marina View
Asia Square Tower 2
T 6922 6888
www.thewestinsingapore.com

WALLPAPER* CITY GUIDES

Executive Editor
Jeremy Case

Author
Daven Wu

Deputy Editor
Belle Place

Photography Editor
Rebecca Moldenhauer

Junior Art Editor
Jade R Arroyo

Editorial Assistant
Charlie Monaghan

Contributors
Elena Gusperti
Mandy Tie

Intern
Meenu Bhardwaj

Production Controller
Nick Seston

**Marketing & Bespoke
Projects Manager**
Nabil Butt

Wallpaper*® is a
registered trademark
of Time Inc (UK)

First published 2006
Sixth edition 2017

© Phaidon Press Limited

All prices and venue
information are correct
at time of going to press,
but are subject to change.

Original Design
Loran Stosskopf
Map Illustrator
Russell Bell

Contacts
wcg@phaidon.com
@wallpaperguides

More City Guides
www.phaidon.com/travel

PHAIDON

Phaidon Press Limited
Regent's Wharf
All Saints Street
London N1 9PA

Phaidon Press Inc
65 Bleecker Street
New York, NY 10012

Phaidon® is a registered
trademark of Phaidon
Press Limited

www.phaidon.com

A CIP Catalogue record for
this book is available from
the British Library.

All rights reserved.
No part of this publication
may be reproduced, stored
in a retrieval system or
transmitted, in any form
or by any means,
electronic, mechanical,
photocopying, recording
or otherwise, without
the prior permission of
Phaidon Press.

Printed in China

ISBN 978 0 7148 7382 4

PHOTOGRAPHERS

Marc Tan
Singapore city view,
inside front cover
People's Park Complex,
p013
Amoy Hotel, p017
Lloyd's Inn, pp018-019
The Club, p026, p027
Oasia Hotel Downtown,
p030, p031
Summer Pavilion, p035
Potato Head Folk, p038
Whitegrass, p041
Jaan, p044
Stella at 1-Altitude, p045
Hashida Sushi, pp046-047
Chopsuey Café, pp050-051
Violet Oon, p055
Open Farm Community,
p060
Dawn Ng, p063
FOST Gallery, p067
Gajah Gallery, p069
Supreme Court, p085
In Good Company, p093
Onlewo, p094
Tarte, p095

Darren Soh
Marina Bay Sands/Helix
Bridge, pp010-011
ION Orchard, p012
The Ritz-Carlton, p021
Regent, p024
Capella, p025
Gardens by the Bay, p036
AXA Life Building, p073

Iwan Baan
The Interlace, pp074-075

Douglas Friedman
StraitsKitchen, p049
Assyafaah Mosque,
pp086-087

Tim Griffith
Church of St Mary of the
Angels, p080, p081

Hufton and Crow
Learning Hub, NTU,
pp082-083

Andrew Rowat
Pearl Bank, p014, p015

Derek Swalwell
National Mosque, Kuala
Lumpur, p099

Wizards of Light
Tanjong Beach Club, p048

Ying Yi
The Ritz-Carlton, p020
The Intan, p033
Horse's Mouth Bar,
p052, p053
Restaurant André,
pp056-057
Oxwell & Co, p058
Gillman Barracks, p066
ArtScience Museum, p084

SINGAPORE
A COLOUR-CODED GUIDE TO THE HOT 'HOODS

ORCHARD ROAD
A paean to the mall, one-stop shopping doesn't come any easier than along this artery

TANJONG PAGAR
The markets, boutiques and happening clubs in this buzzy quarter attract the cool crowd

RAFFLES PLACE
High-rises, government buildings, theatres and hotels cluster around the Singapore River

LITTLE INDIA
It's Disney does Delhi, as if industrial cleaners have been in to tidy up the subcontinent

BALESTIER
Colonial chic and leafy lanes make this suburb an escape from the hustle and bustle

KATONG
If you want to see what Singapore looked like before the skyscrapers, head here fast

For a full description of each neighbourhood, see the Introduction.
Featured venues are colour-coded, according to the district in which they are located.